WOW! PIRATES
I didn't know that

The first pirate to spot a sail on the horizon was rewarded with the best weapon they could steal.

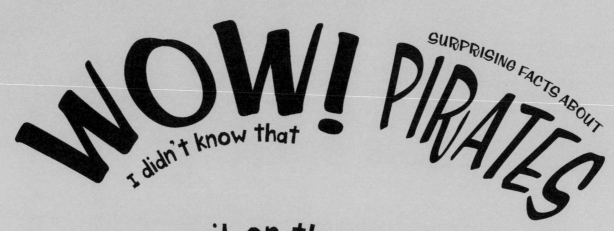

KINGFISHER
LONDON & NEW YORK

Copyright © Macmillan Children's Books 2014
Published in the United States by Kingfisher,
175 Fifth Ave., New York, NY 10010
Kingfisher is an imprint of Macmillan Children's Books, London.

Author: Philip Steele
Editor: Carron Brown
Design and styling: Amy McSimpson
Jacket design: Mike Davis
Illustrations: Marc Aspinall

Distributed in the U.S. and Canada by Macmillan, 175 Fifth Ave., New York, NY 10010

Library of Congress Cataloging-in-Publication data has been applied for.

ISBN 978-0-7534-7188-3 (HB)
ISBN 978-0-7534-7189-0 (PB)

Kingfisher books are available for special promotions and premiums.
For details contact: Special Markets Department, Macmillan, 175 Fifth Ave., New York, NY 10010.

For more information, please visit www.kingfisherbooks.com

Printed in China
1 3 5 7 9 8 6 4 2
1TR/0614/WKT/UG/140WF

WOW! I didn't know that PIRATES

SURPRISING FACTS ABOUT

The youngest known pirate was John King, aged 11, whose ship sank in a storm off Cape Cod in 1717.

KINGFISHER

NEW YORK

The word "pirate" was first used by the ancient Greeks, around 2,500 years ago. It meant attacker.

Pirates have had many names, including corsairs, buccaneers, freebooters, and filibusters.

There were around 1,000 to 2,000 pirates in the Caribbean Sea at any one time from the 1600s to the 1700s.

Privateers were sailors who had permission from their government to attack enemy ships. They were still mean and murderous.

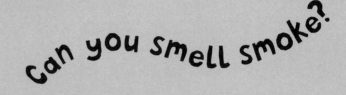

Can you smell smoke?

Some important people (such as rich merchants and politicians) secretly sponsored pirate voyages and enjoyed a share of the treasure.

Viking treasure seekers with scary nicknames like "Bloodax" or "Skullsplitter" raided seaside villages.

A monk named Eustace was an English Channel pirate. He was captured in 1217 and had his head chopped off.

In the 1720s, daring Welsh pirate Black Bart Roberts liked a refreshing cup of hot tea after a hard day's fighting.

6

In the 1690s, the French pirate Antonio Fuët was a real showoff. He fired gold coins at his enemy when he ran out of cannonballs.

BOOM!

Around 300 years ago, Captain Edward Teach, known as Blackbeard, tied smoking cords into his long, tangled hair to scare people.

In the 1650s, buccaneer captain Pierre le Grand drilled a hole in his boat so that his men would attack another ship before theirs sank. The ship that they attacked was full of treasure.

The first buccaneers attacked large ships called galleons from small canoes. This was a good plan since these small boats were hard to hit with cannonballs.

The Welsh adventurer Henry Morgan led huge pirate armies to attack the Spanish. In 1668, he captured Portobello in Panama. His men took just eight days to strip the town of its treasure.

Bartolomeu Portugues was a bad swimmer. He escaped from an enemy by using big clay jars to keep him afloat until he kicked his way to the shore.

I surrender!

One trick was to sneak up behind a galleon and jam its rudder. Once the ship couldn't turn, the pirates swarmed aboard.

Port Royal, Jamaica, home to many pirates, was destroyed in 1692 by an earthquake. People said that this was punishment for its wicked ways.

The first buccaneers lived on the Caribbean islands of Hispaniola and Tortuga. They hunted wild pigs and cattle.

Catch that pig!

Many sailors believed that it was unlucky to set sail with a lady on board. Even so, some of the wildest pirates were women.

The lives of Anne Bonny and Mary Read were spared when they were captured because they were expecting babies.

Anne Cormac married a pirate named James Bonny and then ran off with another pirate named "Calico Jack" Rackham. She was a fierce fighter.

From the 1560s, Grace O'Malley was the Irish pirate queen of Clew Bay. Her crews attacked many English ships.

Mary Read pretended to be a man so that she could be a soldier. Mary joined Calico Jack's pirate crew when he captured her ship in the Caribbean.

The most powerful female pirate was Zheng Yi Sao. She commanded more than 80,000 pirates in the South China Sea in the 1800s.

squeak!

If pirates planned to steal a ship, they tried not to damage it during a battle.

Viking raiders used wooden longships, which were built for speed. Just the sight of their sails caused terror.

Most pirates used any ships that they could steal—the faster, the better!

The Barbary pirates had fast ships called galleys, which were powered by oars and a sail. They were rowed by up to 90 slaves.

In 1696, Captain William Kidd sailed a galley that could reach a speed of 14 knots (17 mph, or 27km/h) using all of its sails and a fair wind.

"sail on..."

Warships of the 1300s had two high fighting decks called castles. The guns were badly made and often exploded when cannons were fired from them.

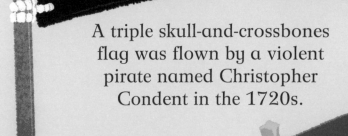

A triple skull-and-crossbones flag was flown by a violent pirate named Christopher Condent in the 1720s.

Pirate flags were later called "jolly rogers" or "blackjacks."

Pirates often flew flags to trick people. They would sail up to a merchant ship, while flying the flag of a friendly country. Only at the last moment would they hoist the jolly roger.

Black Bart Roberts' flag showed a pirate captain greeting a skeleton.

Whoosh!

Blackbeard's flag was one of the scariest. It featured a skeleton aiming a spear at a bleeding heart.

Instead of bones, Calico Jack's blackjack design had swords called cutlasses.

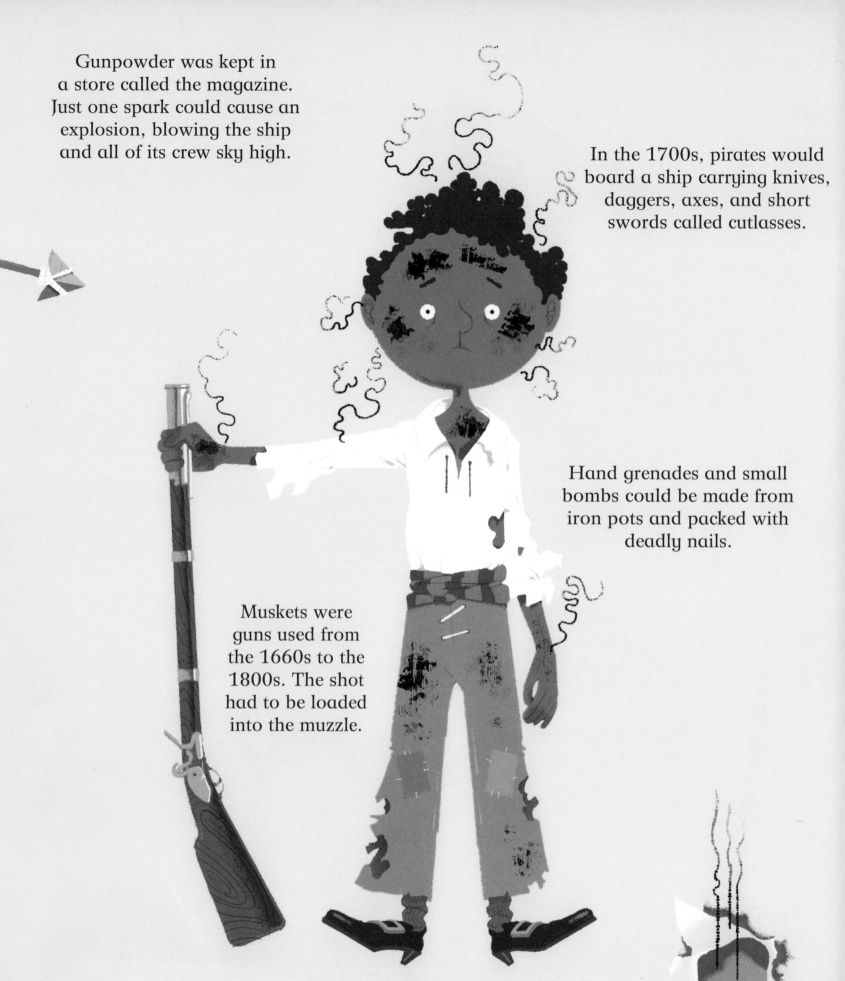

Gunpowder was kept in a store called the magazine. Just one spark could cause an explosion, blowing the ship and all of its crew sky high.

In the 1700s, pirates would board a ship carrying knives, daggers, axes, and short swords called cutlasses.

Hand grenades and small bombs could be made from iron pots and packed with deadly nails.

Muskets were guns used from the 1660s to the 1800s. The shot had to be loaded into the muzzle.

16

Small boats called fireships were packed with gunpowder and fuses. They were sent toward enemy ships ready to explode.

At short range, pistols were used. They were fired with a gadget called a flintlock, which set off a charge of gunpowder.

Small cannon could fire in a circle, turning on the spot. These weapons killed many sailors along the decks of enemy ships.

Pirates often fought and injured one another. Blackbeard once shot his first mate in the leg, just to prove a point!

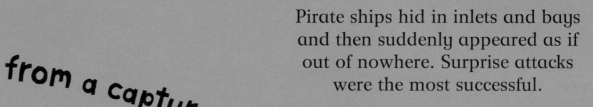

Pirate ships hid in inlets and bays and then suddenly appeared as if out of nowhere. Surprise attacks were the most successful.

Sailors from a captured ship might be forced to join the pirates, especially if they had useful skills, such as carpentry!

Pirates sometimes had spies in taverns and around quaysides and harbors. They found out which ships had precious cargoes and where they were sailing.

Welsh pirate captain Howell Davies once pretended to be a merchant ship captain. As a guest at a meal in an African fort, he took the governor prisoner and stole all of the gold and ivory.

The Spanish thought that pirate Henry Morgan was rowing a huge army ashore from his ship, but it was just the same sailors over and over again. They hid in the bottom of the boat for the return trip.

Sometimes pirates would disguise themselves as harmless passengers. Was that a beard under the old lady's scarf? Or a pair of pistols in that basket? Surely not!

There be treasure!

Pirates stole treasure that was valuable, easy to transport and share among the crew, and easily sold. Gold bars, coins, jewels, or fancy weapons were perfect booty.

Pirates liked stealing items that were useful on their voyage, such as food, drink, maps, tools, telescopes, weapons, and medicine.

Pirates also stole cargoes that would fetch a good price, such as sugar, dyes, spices, and animal skins— but they had to sell these quickly and make their getaway.

From the 1500s, Central and South America were known as the Spanish Main. Famous coins from here included pieces of eight and doubloons.

Pirate maps that mark the site of buried treasure exist only in storybooks.

In 1699, Captain Kidd buried treasure on Gardiners Island, New York. Ever since then people have been searching for buried pirate treasure, without luck.

Captured ships and their precious cargo were often taken over by pirates or added to their fleet. Unwanted ships might be scuttled—sank on purpose.

Blackbeard liked to drink rum, especially when it was sprinkled with a pinch of gunpowder!

Pirates and other seafarers ate a bird called the dodo, which lived on the island of Mauritius. Hunting and the introduction of other animals made the dodo extinct by the 1660s.

On the ship, pirates sometimes kept chickens for their eggs—or "cackle-fruit," as they were known!

During a long voyage, the water could be foul and the only food might be hard, dry biscuits, which were often wriggling with weevils.

In the old days, many seafarers became very sick from a disease called scurvy if they did not eat enough fruit and vegetables.

Pirates loved to feast and drink when they went ashore. That was when fights often broke out.

Fishing was good in tropical seas, and pirates also ate sea turtles. When they went ashore, they hunted monkeys, snakes, and big lizards called iguanas.

Life for normal seafarers
was incredibly harsh long ago.
Sailors often rose up against
their officers in a mutiny.
They took over the ship
and turned to piracy.

Some pirates were
just adventurers who
wanted to sail the
seven seas and win
fame and fortune.

Pirate rules stated how
much a shipmate was to
be paid if he was injured.
For example, if he
lost a leg in battle,
he might be awarded
800 pieces of eight.

A pirate's life was often boring. If no ships
were captured, the decks still had to be
scrubbed and ropes had to be mended.
Pirates had to keep watch for hours on end.

Many pirates were nothing more than crazy murderers and criminals.

Keep walking!

Pirates generally wrote their own rules and elected their own captains.

Some pirates made themselves kings by founding their own kingdoms on the African island of Madagascar. Pirate James Plantain was the king of Ranter Bay from 1715 to 1728.

The most famous pirate punishment is "walking the plank"—forcing victims to walk overboard and plunge into shark-infested waters. This is really a tale from storybooks and not a historical fact.

Pirates punished one another for breaking their agreements and punished any captives who would not do as they were told.

Ancient Greek pirates just tied up their victims and threw them overboard.

Pirates found out if the captain of a captured ship had treated his crew well. If not, he might be flogged or shot in revenge.

Any pirates who did not take care of their weapons were severely punished by their shipmates.

Irish pirate captain Edward England was marooned by his crew. He made a small raft and escaped to Madagascar.

A favorite punishment—for captives or for shipmates—was marooning. The prisoner was left behind on a desert island, with just a little water and a gun for hunting. He might never be rescued.

In 67 B.C.E, a Roman commander named Pompey led a hunt for pirates across the Mediterranean Sea. Thousands of pirates were caught.

Woodes Rogers was a privateer who became a famous pirate hunter in the 1720s. As the governor of the Bahamas, he finally put an end to piracy in the Caribbean.

Grrrr!

In 1840, there was a big battle between a British naval force and a Chinese pirate fleet near Hong Kong.

As long as there have been pirates, they have been hunted down by naval forces, soldiers, or bounty hunters wanting to collect a reward.

In 1718, after a fierce battle, Blackbeard's head was cut off and hung from the front of a ship.

In 1723, a mighty sea battle raged for eight hours off Delaware Bay.

Some people claim to have seen the ghost of Captain Kidd by the Thames River, in London, England. Others say that he haunts Gardiners Island, in New York.

For 400 years, pirates were hanged at London's Execution Dock, beside the Thames River. Captain William Kidd met his end there in 1701.

Pirates' bodies might be displayed to the public, covered in tar, and placed in an iron cage. They were hung up at Rotherhithe or Greenwich, in England as a terrible warning to all sailors leaving the port of London.

Some pirates and privateers used their ill-gotten gains to buy their way into the nobility, with grand houses and fine carriages. Nobody knew about the crimes that they had committed.

Some pirates were sorry for their crimes, but others met their deaths dressed in their finest clothes, joking and laughing with the crowd.

There are still pirates today. Between
2009 and 2012, the European Union's
pirate-hunting patrol took aboard
128 suspected pirates off the
coast of Somalia, in Africa.

Today's pirate treasure includes money, credit cards,
jewelry, expensive watches, and computers.

Modern pirates often use small
boats with powerful motors.
Others may use old
fishing boats so that they
look peaceful.

Pirates in the 21st century
don't use telescopes. They have
the latest high-tech equipment,
from GPS to night-vision goggles.